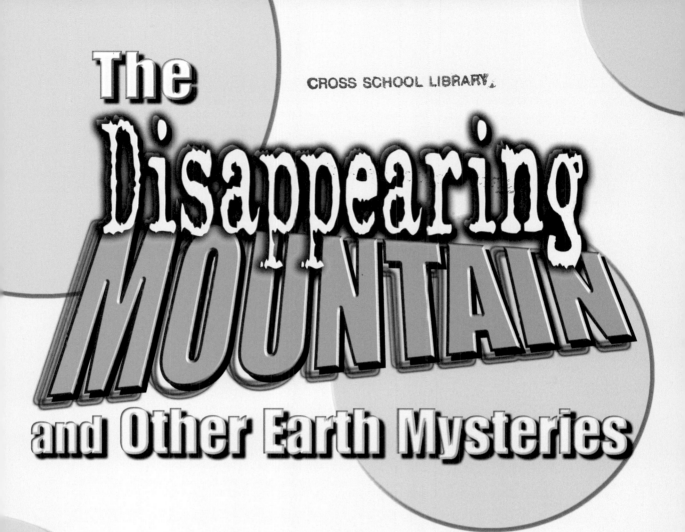

The Disappearing MOUNTAIN

and Other Earth Mysteries

Chicago, Illinois

Raintree

Printed and bound in the United States by Lake Book
Manufacturing, Inc.

10 09 08 07
10 9 8 7 6 5 4 3 2

**Library of Congress Cataloging-in-
Publication Data**
Spilsbury, Louise.
  The disappearing mountain and other earth
mysteries : erosion and
weathering / Louise and Richard Spilsbury.
    p. cm.
  Includes bibliographical references and index.
  ISBN 978-1-4109-1924-3 (1-4109-1924-2) (HC)
  ISBN 978-1-4109-1955-7 (1-4109-1955-2) (Pbk)

  1. Erosion--Juvenile literature. 2. Weathering--
Juvenile literature.
I. Spilsbury, Richard, 1963- II. Title.
  QE571.S687 2005
  551.3'02--dc22
                                        2005009537

Acknowledgments
The author and publishers are grateful to the
following for permission to reproduce copyright
material: Associated Press pp. 10–11 (Kevork
Djansezian), 12–13 (Ben Margot), 26 left (Kevork
Djansezian), 26 bottom (Ben Margot); Corbis pp. 4–5
(Bettman); Corbis Royalty-Free pp. 27 middle, 27
second right, 27 top left, 29 bottom; FLPA pp. 16–17
(Minden Pictures/Tim Fitzharris); Geoscience Features
Picture Library pp. 8–9, 26, 25 top, 29 top; Getty p. 7
top (Photodisc); Getty Images p. 7 bottom (Taxi);
Harcourt Index p. 28 bottom (Corbis); NHPA pp.
20–21 (N.A. Callow), 24–25 (Martin Harvey); Oxford
Scientific Films pp. 14–15 (David Messent), 18–19
(John Downer), 5 bottom (Gilliane Tedder), 7 middle
(Index Stock Photography); Science Photo Library
pp. 22 (Bernhard Edmaier), 23 (Sinclair Stammers),
26r (Bernhard Edmaier), 27b (Sinclair Stammers),
28t (NASA).

Cover photograph of Mount Hood in Oregon, USA,
reproduced with permission of Getty Images/Taxi.

Illustrations by Darren Lingard.

The publishers would like to thank Nancy Harris
and Harold Pratt for their assistance in the
preparation of this book.

Every effort has been made to contact copyright
holders of any material reproduced in this book.
Any omissions will be rectified in subsequent
printings if notice is given to the publishers.

The paper used to print this book comes from
sustainable resources.

Contents

The Mystery Mission   4

A Changing Earth   6

The Disappearing Mountain   8

The Missing Streets   10

The Vanishing House   12

The Shrinking Land   14

The Largest Hole on Earth   16

The Widest Waterfall in the World   18

Strange Carvings in the Rock   20

A Giant's Weapon?   22

Shifting Sands   24

Pieces of the Puzzle   26

More Mysteries to Solve   28

Glossary   30

Want to Know More?   31

Index   32

Some words are printed in bold, **like this**. You can find out what they mean on page 30. You can also look in the box at the bottom of the page where they first appear.

The Mystery Mission

Earth's surface is changing all the time. Huge mountains disappear. Rocks form strange shapes. Hills of sand come and go. In the past, people made up stories to explain these mysteries. Your mission is to find out the facts.

What made this giant hole in the ground? This is an easy mystery to solve. People have been digging rocks out of the ground for more than 100 years. The people want the copper, silver, and gold that are in the rock.

But people are not the cause of the other Earth mysteries in this book . . .

Can you dig it?

Bingham Canyon Copper Mine is in Utah. It is the biggest human-made hole in the world. You could lay more than 25 football fields across it!

Diggers like these made the giant hole. They drive into the open-pit mine along the long tracks you can see in the main picture.

A Changing Earth

Water, wind, and ice are forces of nature. They can change and shape Earth's **landforms**. Hills and mountains are types of landform.

Weathering is the wearing away of rock. Wind, ice, and flowing water can cause weathering. They break the rock into tiny pieces. These tiny pieces get washed or blown away to another place. The movement is called **erosion**.

Sometimes we can see changes as they happen. A storm can quickly blow away part of a sandy beach. Yet most changes happen too slowly for us to see them. We need to use clues in the landforms to find out why they have changed.

Ice can break rock ▶
into small pieces.

erosion	movement of rock and soil from place to place
landform	mountains and other features of Earth's surface
weathering	when rock is broken down by the weather

Strong winds ▶
can slowly wear
away rocks.

◀ Water can move small
pieces of rock.

The Disappearing Mountain

You may have heard of mountain climbers disappearing.
Yet have you ever heard of a mountain disappearing?

Hills and mountains are not solid lumps of rock that never change. The wind and rain can change the shape of hills and mountains. **Weathering** can make hills and mountains get smaller. It can take millions of years to wear away a mountain!

How can rain and ice make a mountain disappear? Look at the clues to get to the bottom of this mystery.

1) Rain gets into cracks in rocks. The rain turns to ice when it gets cold. Ice takes up more space than water. Ice makes the cracks in rocks get bigger.

scree   small, loose stones on a mountain slope

2) These bits of broken stone are called **scree**. Rain and ice slowly break large rocks into scree. This is how the mountain disappears.

Th Missing Stre ts

Yesterday, these streets were full of houses and people.
Today, some of the houses and people have vanished.

The town was hit by a **mudflow**. A mudflow happens
when a lot of **sediment** (soil) suddenly moves downhill.
This mudflow buried everything in its path. Now, the
mud has set. It is as dry and hard as concrete.

Where did the mud come from? Look at the clues
to get to the bottom of this mystery.

1) Rain, wind, and ice break rocks into
small pieces. The small pieces of rock
are called sediment. Sediment makes
up a large part of soil.

2) Soil soaks up rainwater
like a sponge. The rainwater
turns the soil into mud.

mudflow   when wet soil flows downhill
sediment   very tiny pieces of rock or shells, such as sand or mud

3) Mountains have sloping sides. Wet soil can slip down mountains. The mud has buried some of the buildings in this town.

The Vanishing House

One minute, a house and garden were on this spot. The next minute, they were gone.

The house and garden fell into a **sinkhole**. Every year, there are reports of sinkholes in U.S. newspapers. Houses, roads, and cars are suddenly swallowed up by Earth.

There is no warning that sinkholes are going to happen. The land feels solid and safe. Then, suddenly a sinkhole appears.

How does **weathering** cause sinkholes? Look at the clues to get to the bottom of this mystery.

1) Some houses are built on soft, crumbly rock. Rainwater can get underground and **dissolve** rocks like this. The rock is broken down by the water. The water drains away and leaves a sinkhole.

dissolve when a solid breaks down into a liquid
sinkhole large hole in the ground that opens suddenly

2) The soft rock slowly dissolves away. Large holes are left underground. This takes thousands of years. The land above the holes cannot support the houses. The houses fall into the hole.

The Shrinking Land

There are warning signs at the top of this cliff. The signs tell people to keep away from the edge. There is a risk of a **landslide**. The edge of the cliff could break away, slide, and crash into the sea.

The land is shrinking. Chunks of rock are slowly breaking off. They fall into the sea. Landslides make large parts of the cliff disappear.

Why are these landslides happening? Use the clues to find out.

1) Waves crash against the bottom of the cliffs. The waves slowly wear away the bottom of the cliff.

landslide	when rock or soil slides down a slope
erode	move or carry away bits of rock

2) The top of the cliff is left hanging. Bits of rock collapse. They fall down onto the shore. A landslide happens when a lot of rocks suddenly fall at once.

3) Waves knock the bits of rock against each other. This **weathering** breaks the bits of rock into smaller pieces. Then, the waves carry away pieces of rock. The waves **erode** the cliff.

The Largest Hole on Earth

You are looking down at the biggest **canyon** on Earth. The Grand Canyon in Arizona is more than 277 miles (445 kilometers) long. It is 15 miles (24 kilometers) wide and 1 mile (1.8 kilometers) deep in places.

The water running along the bottom of the Grand Canyon is the Colorado River. The Colorado River created the Grand Canyon.

How has water flowing downhill created the Grand Canyon? Look at the clues to find out.

1) The river moves fast as it flows downhill. The water is heavy and powerful. It **weathers** the land as it flows along. It crumbles off bits of rock.

canyon very deep valley with steep sides, carved by a river
valley place where a river has cut down into the ground

2) Moving water **erodes**, or moves, rocks. The small pieces of rock are dragged along by the river. They help the river to scratch deeper into the land. Rivers can slowly make deep **valleys**. Very deep valleys are called canyons.

17

The Widest Waterfall in the World

Victoria Falls is in Africa. It is one of the widest waterfalls in the world. It is 1 mile (1.7 kilometers) across.

Why does the river suddenly drop into this huge hole in the land? Look at the clues to solve the mystery.

ledge   river flow

soft rock   hard rock

1) Moving water **weathers** and **erodes** soft rock faster than hard rock. The river slowly cuts down into the soft rock. It creates a ledge. This takes thousands of years.

2) The river flows over the ledge. The falling water is very heavy and powerful. It wears away more rock. The hole becomes deeper and wider. It forms a waterfall.

19

Strange Carvings in the Rock

How was this strange shape made in the desert rocks? Maybe it was carved by people?

In fact, this shape was carved by water. The shape is called an arch. A long time ago, a small river flowed here. Look at the photo to find out how the river carved the arch.

2) There were small pieces of rock in the river. These small pieces scratched away at the solid rock. More scratching happened near the bottom of the river than near the surface.

1) Long ago, the hole in the arch was solid rock. The river flowed around this solid rock.

3) The water broke off small pieces of rock as it flowed. This is called **weathering**. Pieces of the solid rock broke off on both sides. Eventually, the arch was formed.

A Giant's Weapon.

This rock is in the middle of nowhere. It is a different kind of rock from the other rocks in the area. This is because it came from a long way away.

The rock is far too heavy for rivers to carry or wind to blow it. So, how did it get here?

An old story says that an angry giant threw the rock here. In fact, the rock was moved here by a **glacier**. A glacier is a slow-moving sheet of ice. A glacier passed through this place thousands of years ago. The rock has been left here because of **deposition**. Read the clues to find out how this happened.

1) Rocks are picked up by a glacier as it moves along. The glacier drops the rocks as it melts. This is called deposition. Deposition leaves the rocks far from where they originally came.

deposition   when rock or sediment is dropped in a new place
glacier   huge, slow-moving sheet of ice

2) The shape of a **landform** can show if a glacier passed over it. Glaciers carve out smooth, U-shaped **valleys** as they slide along.

Shifting Sands

It is hard to find your way around an open desert. You cannot use the sand **dunes** as landmarks. These hills of sand move all the time. Some sand dunes move or form new shapes in just a few days.

How do sand dunes change so quickly? Look at the clues to find out!

1) A fast wind can **erode**, or move, a lot of sand. Small grains of sand are blown around in the air. Big grains of sand are blown along the ground.

Can sand dunes sing?

Sand dunes sometimes make a sound like the hum of a distant airplane. The sand grains rub against each other to make the sound.

deposit to put or set down rock or sediment in a new place
dune hill of sand piled up by the wind

2) The wind slows down when it blows past a rock or a plant. It drops some of the sand. The sand it **deposits** makes a little pile. This little pile gets bigger. Slowly, it forms a sand dune.

Pieces of the Puzzle

Good detectives look for links between mysteries. You have looked at different Earth mysteries in this book. What links them together?

The answer is **weathering**, **erosion,** and **deposition**. Weathering wears down rocks into pieces. Erosion carries these pieces away. The pieces might get carried away by moving water, the wind, or something else. Deposition is when the pieces are dropped in a new place.

Weathering:

Weathering and erosion:

Erosion and deposition:

These processes change the surface of our planet. We can solve Earth mysteries. But we cannot stop them from happening. The forces of nature are too powerful!

Mor Mysteries to Solve

New Earth mysteries come in all the time. Here are some extra case files for you. You know what clues to look for. There are some notes to help you, too.

The delta

This photo has been taken from space. It shows the place where the Mississippi River flows into the sea. Yet why is the seawater a different color near the river?

An enormous rock

This is the famous Ayer's Rock in Australia. The red rock is very hard. Why does it stick up above the rest of the land?

The crumbling face

This stone carving was on the outside of a building lashed by rain. Why are its forehead and cheek missing?

A doorway in the sea

What could the waves in the bottom of this picture have to do with this wonderful arch of rock?

An enormous rock

The soft rock around Ayer's Rock has slowly been **eroded**. The red rock is much harder. The red rock hasn't been eroded.

The delta

The river has picked up **sediment** and rocks as it flowed toward the sea. The sediment and rocks are carried along by the water. They are then **deposited** when the river flows into the sea.

A doorway in the sea

The powerful waves have weathered and eroded parts of the rock to form an arch.

The crumbling face

The power of the rain has slowly **weathered** the statue. Parts of the rock have been **dissolved** and washed away.

Glossary

canyon very deep valley with steep sides, carved by a river. The Grand Canyon is the most famous canyon in the world.

deposit to put or set down rock or sediment in a new place

deposition when rock or sediment is dropped in a new place. A beach is one example of deposition.

dissolve when a solid breaks down into a liquid. Salt dissolves in water.

dune hill of sand piled up by the wind. Dunes are found in deserts and on beaches.

erode move or carry away bits of rock. Waves slowly erode rocks from the base of cliffs.

erosion movement of rock from place to place. Flowing water and wind can cause erosion.

glacier huge, slow-moving sheet of ice. Glaciers form in cold places, such as high mountains.

landform mountains and other features of Earth's surface

landslide when rock or soil slide down a slope. Some landslides happen when bits of rock from the top of a cliff fall down to the shore.

mudflow when wet soil flows downhill. Mudflows often happen after heavy rainfall.

scree small, loose stones on a mountain slope. Scree is formed when ice breaks up mountain rocks.

sediment very tiny pieces of rock or shells, such as sand or mud. Weathering forms sediment.

sinkhole large hole in the ground that opens suddenly. Sinkholes are often found in areas of limestone rock.

valley place where a river has cut down into the ground. Valleys have sloping sides.

weathering when rock is broken down by the weather. Weathering can change the surface of Earth.

Want to Know More?

Books

- Colson, Mary. *Crumbling Earth*. Chicago: Raintree, 2004.

- Spilsbury, Louise and Richard. *Thundering Landslides*. Chicago: Heinemann Library, 2004.

- Weintraub, Aileen. *The Grand Canyon: Widest Canyon*. New York: Rosen, 2000.

Websites

- http://www.nationalgeographic.com/grandcanyon/kids.html
  Visit this website to find out more about the Grand Canyon. You can learn about animals that live in the Grand Canyon and take a cool quiz! Sponsored by National Geographic.

- http://www.fema.gov/kids/
  Do you want to learn more about the different types of natural disasters and how you can be prepared for them? Check out this exciting website to play games and take quizzes! Sponsored by the Federal Emergency Management Agency.

Learn about the life of a piece of rock in *Tales of a Prehistoric Sponge*.

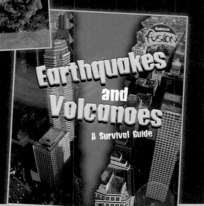

Read *Earthquakes and Volcanoes: A Survival Guide* to find out how terrifying Earth's processes can be.

Index

arches 21, 29

Ayer's Rock 28–29

Bingham Canyon Copper Mine 4

canyons 16–17

cliffs 14–15

deltas 28–29

deposition 22, 25–27, 29

dissolve 12, 29

dunes 24–25

erode/erosion 6, 14–15, 17–18, 20–21, 23–24, 26–27, 29

glaciers 22–23

Grand Canyon 16–17

hills and mountains 4, 6, 8–9, 11

ice 6, 8–10, 22

landforms 6, 23

landslides 14–15

mines 4–5

mudflows 10–11

rainwater 8–10, 12–13, 29

rivers 16–19, 28–29

rocks 4, 6–7, 10, 12, 14–18, 20–22, 25–26, 28–29

sand 4, 6, 20–21, 24–25

scree 8–9

sediment 10, 20–21, 29

sinkholes 12–13

valleys 16–17, 23

Victoria Falls 18–19

water 6–10, 12–16, 18–19, 29

waterfalls 18–19

waves 14–15, 29

weathering 6, 8, 12, 15–16, 18, 20–21, 26–27, 29

wind 6–8, 10, 20–21, 24–25